IMAGES
of America

GLENSHAW

IMAGES
of America

GLENSHAW

Violet Rowe

ARCADIA

First published 1997
Copyright © Violet Rowe, 1997

ISBN 0-7524-0944-1

Published by Arcadia Publishing,
an imprint of the Chalford Publishing Corporation,
One Washington Center, Dover, New Hampshire 03820.
Printed in Great Britain

Library of Congress Cataloging-in-Publication Data applied for

Contents

Introduction

This book covers pictures of the Glenshaw area from 1800 to about the 1940s. It shows what the area, the people, and the industries looked like then, and how the community has grown.

When Shaler Township was incorporated in 1837, it had a population of 2,000. By 1860 the population was 16,399. Its present population is 33,000.

In 1800, John Shaw Sr. purchased 600 acres of land just 8 miles north of the city of Pittsburgh in Shaler Township. He built a log sawmill to prepare the lumber for his home. Later, Shaw built a log gristmill, which stood until 1845, when his son built a larger gristmill. This new mill stood on the property across from the Glenshaw School, in an area called Shaw's Glen.

I am going to quote from Sylvester Wagner's "My Childhood Memory Sketches," which is dated June 1, 1944. These quoted paragraphs best describes the Glenshaw that is shown in this book.

"Glenshaw was a very small town with not too many people. There was plenty of wide open spaces and quite a few farms. We had a general store—Edgar's—and a post office, and a public school, a railroad station, and one of the first public libraries. There was also a gas station with one hand pump and free air. Glenshaw was on both sides of Route 8, the main road leading north. Etna was our neighbor town to the south. There was two parts to Glenshaw, Upper Glenshaw and Lower Glenshaw. Lower Glenshaw, where I lived, consisted of Sourkraut Row, the Flats, and Tony Town. The Shaw homestead was in Lower Glenshaw, and from these early settlers the town was named 'Glenshaw, or Shaw's Glen.' Upper Glenshaw, which ran from present day Undercliff Fire Company to St. Bonaventure Church. In between these two landmarks lay the farms of the Braun family, the Hoffman's, the Bustler's, the Wetzel's, the Schmidt's, the Christof's and the McClure's. The McClure farm was also known as the Stock Farm, because there always was a lot of cattle grazing there to become fat before being sent to the slaughterhouse. Jr. McClure had a hired tenant family that worked the one hundred or so acres he owned adjacent to Mt. Royal Blvd. The family who ran his farm was named Carrigen and during the influenza plague of 1918, Mrs. Carrigan and 7 of the 10 children died. Mr. Carrigan moved to a different locale shortly after and the farm went to pot after that. The large brick homestead is still occupied and is located across from 'North Hills Library.'

"Heading north out of Etna, about 1930, the back way was along Little Pine Creek Rd. It started at Wilson Street and ended at the Cristof and Wetzel farms. Here it turned into Wetzel Road and this road ended up on Mt. Royal Blvd. There was two things memorable about this road. First at Beyerle Avenue there was a huge icehouse owned by Ralph Beyerle. He had large ice ponds alongside the creek, and he cut and stored the ice blocks all winter.

"The most popular swimming hole was Locust Grove, where the K-Mart sits today. The next was the dam at Glenshaw Glass. This place was always crowded and all had a good time frolicking in the water. A lot of the mothers would sit on the bank to make sure no one drowned. Another swimming hole was behind Ball Chemical, where the water washed a hole in the creek about 30 feet long and 4 feet deep. Only boys went there because we could swim naked. Next was Bick's Pond right above the Shaw home. Here the creek was about 30 feet wide and one side it had a sandy beach caused by a back water eddy when the creek was swollen. Locust Grove started out as a picnic grove, but very few picnic's were held there. Later on the owner turned the grove into a trailer park, the first one in all of North Hills.

"When Mt. Royal Blvd. left Etna, it traveled straight up the hill to Reese Avenue. At this point, it made a 90 degree left turn and continued up to the top of the hill. This little town where the road made the sharp left turn was called Reeseville. The present Mt. Royal Blvd. from Beyerle Avenue to the top of Gibson Hill is laid down over the top of the old Butler Short Line's right of way. First was the Braun farm apple orchard, where you were welcome to take anything that was laying on the ground. Next was the Braun School, and next to the school was a mom and pop grocery store run by Mr. & Mrs. Zucharo. Across the street was Fodi's grocery and delicatessen store. Mr. Fodi was one of the founding fathers of the Undercliff Volunteer Fire Department. Just past the corner of Glenn Avenue was Joseph Fasone's grocery store. A half block north was Pearce's Drug Store. Next to Pearce's was Pete Kay's grocery store. He had a truck and would deliver your groceries to your door. He took phone orders in the morning and delivered in the afternoon. next was the Bustler place. When Bill died, the homestead was purchased by Henry Bock.

"From Glenshaw Avenue to the end of Mt. Royal Blvd. there was not much, but some nice buckeye trees between Kleber's dairy and the Vilsack farm. At Elfinwild there was the Hugh barn that was used by Mt. Royal Cemetery as a storage area and the small office that was used to run the cemetery. Across the street was Herman Cohen's store."

This passage sums up what Glenshaw was like in the 1930s, through the eyes of a young boy.

Like Sylvester Wagner, Arthur J. (Pete) McMaster grew up on Glenshaw Avenue, and he became a photographer. He now lives in Shawnee Mission, Kansas. He was a big help in providing many pictures of the 1930s and 1940s. Those who provided pictures are the Glenshaw Public Library, the Shaler Historical Society, Shirley Anderson, Libs MacDonald, Sally Rowley, Sylvia Ferrari Moran, Sylvester Wagner, Marylou Letterle, Jean Cook, Grace McGoun, Betty Kapphan, Verna Hunter Milbert, Carol Schrieber, Lillian Romano, and Phillip Breidenbach.

One
Glenshaw Scenes

In this 1905 bird's-eye view of Glenshaw, the Glenshaw School can be seen, as well as the homes on Glenshaw Avenue and Charles Street.

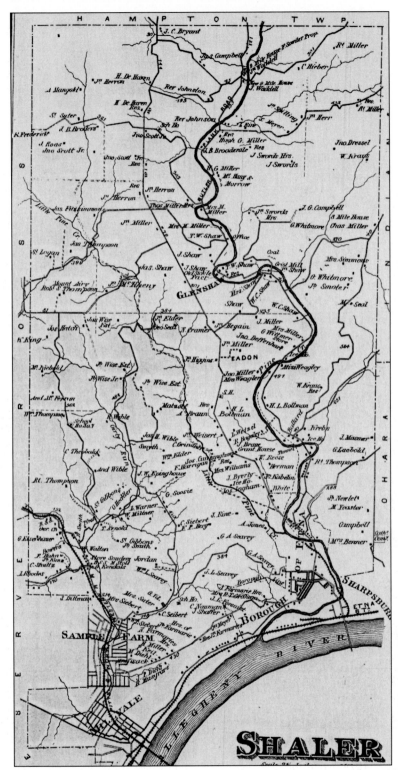

This map of Shaler Township shows the Glenshaw area as it appeared in 1876.

Mary Simmons was born in a log cabin on the site of the railroad station. The frame building to the left was the general store, which was owned by Mr. Frank McMillan. The brick building near the center was a flour and grain mill operated by Mr. John Shaw. The course of the millrace is visible as coming under the railroad tracks. The photograph was taken in 1880.

In 1913, the Glenshaw Library was moved to a room in the I.W. Edgar Building, where it remained until 1924, when the books were returned to the "White Elephant." The post office was also housed in this building.

This photograph shows the Butler Plank Road before the road was paved. The Edgar Building can be seen here, as well as Kay's ice cream store. To the right is the drive to Glenshaw School.

This is a closer view of the Edgar Building. Kay's ice cream store and other buildings are visible farther down Butler Plank Road.

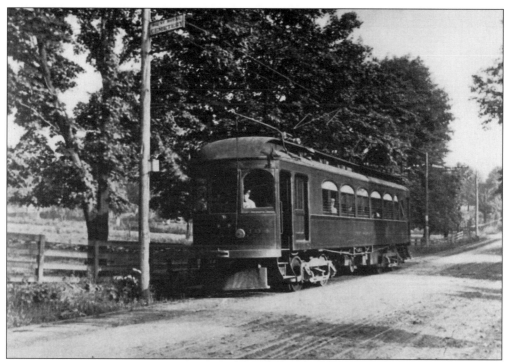

The Butler Short Line streetcar stopped at Mount Royal Boulevard, formerly the Pittsburgh and Butler Turnpike, built in 1822.

Pictured here is a passenger bus from the 1900s.

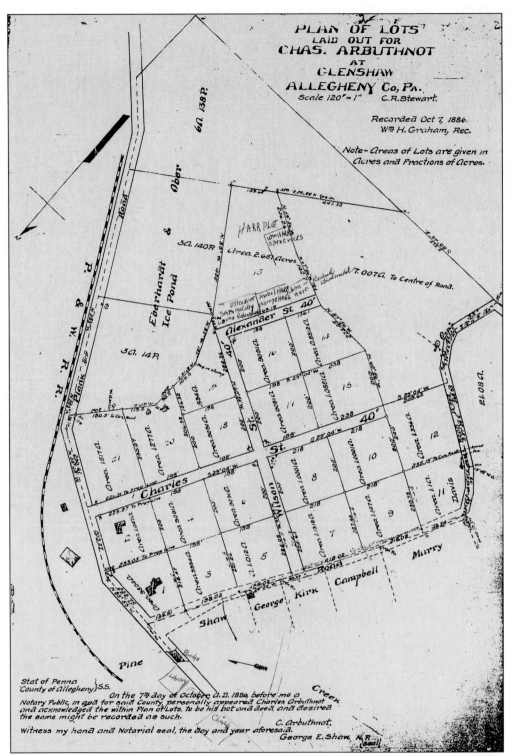

Shown here is the plan of lots laid out for Charles Arbuthnot in 1886. He named the streets for his three sons: Charles, Wilson, and Alexander.

This view of Butler Plank Road, taken in 1909, shows the Glenshaw Public Library, the bridge over Pine Creek, and the Glenshaw Valley Presbyterian Church in the distance.

A bird's-eye view of the Dehaven section of Shaler Township.

This view of Allison Park, taken in 1911, shows Duncan Avenue and St. Ursula's Church.

16

This photograph of the ice gorge at Undercliff was taken on Sunday, February 18, 1912.

This view of the ice gorge on Pine Creek at Glenshaw was taken on February 25, 1912.

The ice on Pine Creek, just below the Glenshaw Valley Presbyterian Church, was captured in this photograph taken on February 12, 1912.

This February 25, 1912 photograph shows the Butler Plank Road covered in ice, with the Shaw home on the right.

In this snow scene of Charles Street, the Glenshaw School can be seen in the upper part of the photograph.

Note the horse and buggy in this early spring view of Charles Street.

This picture, taken in 1928 by Mr. Carl Hoberg, shows a section of Mt. Royal Boulevard extending from Wetzel Road on the left, then Ellen Street, and Hoffman Road. Across Mt. Royal Boulevard is Glenshaw Avenue. The Zeuger home is near the top of the picture. Above and to the right of the Zeuger home is Glenshaw School and Butler Plank Road. The Bustler home, now Bock's Funeral Home, is to the right of Glenshaw Avenue, and next to it is Pierce's Drug Store.

This picture shows the new Glenshaw Presbyterian Church, which was built on Glenn Avenue in 1928 at a cost of $27,000. Pennsylvania Avenue is just below the church.

The bridge over Pine Creek at Fall Run Road was built in 1886. It was replaced in the 1990s and donated to the Montour Rails to Trails committee for use on a bicycle trail.

In downtown Glenshaw in 1938, the garage sign read, "Turner and Grob," and Atlantic White Flash gasoline was the fuel of choice here. Kay's Confectionary Store was next door, and beyond Kay's was Tony Wagner's Meat Market (not visible in this picture). The Edgar Building contained the post office and grocery store, and upstairs were the telephone offices. Beyond that building was Mary Simmon's house.

This photograph shows Glenshaw Valley Church in the winter.

This photograph shows Glenshaw Avenue as it appeared on February 22, 1924.

This view of Butler Plank Road looks over the Fall Run area.

The railroad tracks, Butler Plank Road, and Old Kleber Road are shown here as they appeared before 1940. The Bicks farm is on the hillside.

This photograph shows the ravine, otherwise known as Glenn Avenue, as it appeared to residents in early 1900s.

Seen here in this 1936 photograph are the Butler Plank Road and the Bicks farm. Today it is the site of the Glenshaw Post Office, at the bottom of Kleber Road.

PHOTO BY A. J. McMASTI

In this aerial view, taken in the 1940s of lower Glenshaw, Route 8 is at the top left, then the railroad, and then Butler Plank Road. The Glenshaw Valley Church is visible at the bottom left, and Glenshaw Avenue is in the middle of the picture.

A hike to the Falls was a favorite Sunday afternoon pastime in this late 1930s. Here, Mary Young and Edna McMasters view this beautiful natural scene.

The "Big Rock," an ice age remnant, was a favorite stopping point going up Fall Run on the way to the Falls. From left to right are: (front row) Mary Young, Edna McMasters, Anne McMasters, and an unknown young woman and man; (back row) John Beiswenger, Betty Garrard, Florence McMasters, and an unknown lady in a pillbox hat.

Left: The Falls in Fall Run Park is a natural 25-foot waterfall centrally located in the park. This photograph was taken May 22, 1949.

Right: This view of the Falls, seen from another angle, was taken the same day as the photograph on the upper left.

Left: The "Big Rock" is located in Fall Run Park, which is 1 mile long and no more than 200 to 300 feet wide, with steep sidewalls, some cliff-like, which are 75 to 100 feet high.

Right: This is another photograph of the "Big Rock."

As these photographs show, the Falls in Fall Run Park were a popular spot for taking pictures.

SERVICE MEN
PICK-UP STATION
ROUTE #8 - - - ETNA, PA.

This servicemen's pickup station was erected by the men of the Etna volunteer fire department at Hose House #2, Route 8, Etna.

Shown here are the extraordinarily high waters of Pine Creek as viewed from the Fall Run area on March 3, 1904.

This is another view of Pine Creek's floodwater.

The floodwater of Pine Creek was also captured in this photograph.

This photograph of Hieber's garage was taken from Fall Run.

This is another photograph of Pine Creek.

This is a different view of Pine Creek.

In 1824, Thomas Wilson Shaw built this house, which is now registered with the Pittsburgh History and Landmarks Foundation. The house remained in the Shaw family, with Dr. Katherine Shaw and her sister, Caroline Shaw Tatom, living there until 1990. The two were great-granddaughters of John Shaw.

About 1838, George Vang provided material to build a low-level dam on Pine Creek, across from the Shaw home. This was used for ice skating. The dam was washed out a few years later in one of the floods. Ruth Bullard is standing on the rocks.

A crowd gathered for the dedication of the "new" post office building in June 1942. The post office became a second-class office on July 1, 1945.

The World War II military servicemen were listed on a display in front of the "new" post office in 1944.

This is Route 8 and Butler Plank Road, where the old J & L Warehouse was built.

A hand-pump in the backyard of the Satler house at 901 Glenshaw Avenue provided clear, cool water for passersby. This photograph was taken in 1942.

No. 15   GLENSHAW, PA., THURSDAY, APRIL 9, 1942   Price per copy 5c—$1.50 per

EE SCHOOL DS IN PARADE

A gigantic patriotic parade will find three local high school numbering themselves as marchers as well as the other organizations who participate in the first Victory

parade will commence at 1 p. m.

l Draft Board announces Fourth istration Day Facts

ES MONDAY, APRIL 27

Fourth Registration Day for the Selective Service Act held on Monday, April 27 a. m. to 9 p. m., Clerk Aa Kurtzrock, of Draft Board announces.

registration applies to men to born on or after April 28, 1877 till February 16, 1897.

for the registration have not finitely been ascertained, but and liquor stores will be to the above date.

the Service Headquarters in local boards to start classifi at once of the several million be enrolled on February 16 prepare to fill the Army's June men, and possibly the May b these registrants and regis from the first age group. The count said the "first age designates are remaining the first and second national tions, and men of the "second age" are those who registered 16. Local boards which completed mailing of 88 sure (Form 40) were asked if to all in the first age and at the same time to send registrants in the second age sufficient numbers to insure of the June call (estimat exceed the call of February tirely from this second group, action is required.

local board does not have at number of registrants of age group available in Class fill its call for May 1942, the deliver for induction the from the second age group to fill its call. If the board necessary to furnish men from and age group in May, it continue classification of regis the group to insure that on sufficient number have been to fill a normal call. The ers said the War Depart indicated that beginning quisitions will probably in ed in both age groups, and calls for June and subse nts will be for both groups.

eHaven School PTA Meets

Haven PTA meeting on for Thursday, April 9, at The speaker will be Miss Hunter, the subject, "Sight ion."

ill also be an election of of music.

Hampton Farm-Garden Unit Has Card Party

The Hampton Farm and Garden Club will hold its annual Card Party on April 15 at 8:30 p. m., at the Hampton Consolidated School. Part of the proceeds will be used to pro e for the creating of a scholarship fund for the study of horticulture for some deserving student. Mrs. Paul Yeakle is chairman of the party.

The club will also use some of the e records to buy seeds to be given to the Hampton School students. This year many of them are planning to use their seeds to create little per onal Victory Gardens. Prizes will be awarded for the most satisfactory vegetable and flower garden grown by the students.

On April 15 the club will again present a Gay 90's Show at the School. This show was given a few weeks ago, and is now being repeated in order to raise funds to help defray the cost of equipping an ambulance.

Mrs. Copeland, Mt. Royal Boule vard, was appointed chairman of the show. She is one of the newly elected Vice Presidents of the club, and al ready has done some fine work in the interest of the club. Miss Gertrude M. Bordoner will be Mistress of Ceremonies, and Mrs. Dorothy Mitch ell is director of the show.

Hampton Farm-Garden Club Meets Saturday

The Hampton Farm and Garden Club will hold its monthly meeting on April 11, at the home of Mrs. P E. Hunter, Middle Road.

The club guest and Lawrence "Growing ence is an and has done work in reg

The aides Gestrich, Mrs and Mrs. Bret

Rationing Board Changes Place Of Meeting

NOW AT FIREMENS' BUILDING

The Commodity Rationing Board Number 212, with jurisdiction over Etna, Millvale, Shaler Township, and Reserve Township, which has been meeting at Millvale High School, will meet Fridays at the Millvale Fire Building, from 4 to 6 p. m.

The Board rations tires and auto biles.

The Board wishes to extend thanks through this paper to the Millvale Volunteer Fire Department and the Millvale Council for their coopera tion in getting permanent headquar ters and for providing heat, light, and gas.

Watch this paper for further Board news.

Parent's Magazine Endorses Offense Poster

Reverberations from the publishing of the poster which the VILLAGER editorial was instrumental in chang ing from the negative Defense to the forceful Offense in regard to Savings Bonds and Stamps have included an endorsement by the publisher of the widely known Parent's Magazine, which has announced intentions of publishing the poster in issues.

Red Cross Nutrition Course Lecture

An illustrated lecture on meat by a representative of the Fried and Reineman Company will be given in the Women's Parlor of the Glenshaw Community Church, Friday, April 10 from 7:30 to 9:30 p. m.

All members of the Red Cross Nu trition Group are urged to attend, a representative asks.

Name Local Woman

Walter Lunden, president of rd of managers of the Pitts utheran Inner Mission Soci ve, Etna, as district chair named Mrs. Emilie Bryson, the annual roll call to be ay, April 19th.

old Foster is superintend ociety which is the social cy of 80 Lutheran con Western Pennsylvania.

mages Home

$2,500 damage Satur e of S. E. Tamburo, Park, near the Wild en reported.

GLENSHAW TO GET NEW POST OFFICE BUILDIN

COMPLETION EXPECTED AROUND JUNE

By A. J. McMASTERS

Elementary construction work in preparation for the erection of a n Glenshaw Post Office building has commenc d on a site beside the locati of the present one.

I. W. Edgar, who recently completed 38 years of service as Glensha Postmaster, expects the new building to be completed June 1.

The new building will be fireproof and will occupy the place whe Wagner Brothers Meat Market now stands. The Market is being erected back toward the railroad to allow room for the new building which will approximately 50 feet in length.

The Bell Telephone Company will take over the present post office ba cause of the increasing patronage of the rapidly expanding Glenshaw sub urban area. The telephone company recently took over the entire secon floor of the Edgar General Merchandise Store.

ORIGINALLY ESTABLISHED 185

The first Glenshaw Post Office wa established March 19, 1858, and stoo on the Shaw property at the corner of Glenshaw Avenue and Butler Road William C. Shaw was the first post master.

Originally the mail was brought by way of stage coach which operated between Pittsburgh and Butler. Whe the West Penn Railroad was com pleted to Butler, the stage was no longer used.

In May, 1886, a frame building was built where the present post office is except that it faced north. F. B. Mc Millan was appointed post master May 5, 1886, and he served until March 5, 1904.

The post office was moved on De cember 24, 1887, to a store which Miss Nan Shaw had opened near the present railroad station. Miss Mary Simmons was the clerk.

The present building was erected in 1904 and I. W. Edgar was appoint ed postmaster April 1, 1904.

It was then a fourth class office. January 1, 1921, it was put into the presidential class.

Rapid strides in the growth of rural Glenshaw in the past ten years have made the Glenshaw office very busy, and, no doubt induced plans for the new erection.

Millvale Cadet Killed in Crash

A 24-year-old Millvale army air cadet was Friday when his pla Matagorda Bay, near family was inform

e M. Duvall, of Millvale, was to "wings" and a in two weeks. eatrice Duvall, Good Fellow where he was stationed, the ceremony.

Duvall enlisted in the air corps while a student at Ohio State Uni versity.

Home Nursing Classes Formed in Millvale

Yesterday was the registration date for the organization of Home Nursing Classes, a phase of home defense in Millvale. Both afternoon

Sears of 1942. In out the natio

BEAUT known by the PHYSICAL C

You haven Breads" which t to nothing. The reaso where the cam

 battery on the the skies for enemy bomb , is conceded by those who know what

it necessary to sacrifice something or to give up an insignifi just remember that we're at war.

—30—

Shown here is an article from *The Villager* dealing with the opening of the new post office.

36

Two
Glenshaw Valley Presbyterian Church

In 1835, Thomas Wilson Shaw built a sickle factory on Pine Creek, not far from his home. When the factory ceased to operate, the building became the first Sunday school and church for the Glenshaw Presbyterian Church.

PRES. CHURCH GLENSHAW PA.

The Glenshaw Presbyterian Church was organized in 1885, and the church building was built in 1887 at a cost of $12,000. The church structure is registered with the Pittsburgh History and Landmarks Foundation.

An addition was added to the church in April of 1911. It consisted of a ladies' parlor, a kitchen, and a men's room, and these additions cost $3,000.

This photograph shows the church choir of 1915–1917. From left to right are, as listed on the back of the photograph: John Titzel, Bill Rector, Charles Ross, Floyd Coons, Harry Beiswenger, Howard Dawson, Harry Tedley, Clara Beiswenger, Elizabeth Engelhardt, unidentified, unidentified, Mrs. Blackmore, Edna Ross, unidentified, Laura Hunter, and unidentified.

This church picnic took place at Little Creek in the early 1900s.

The Glenshaw Valley Presbyterian Church

cordially invites you to attend a

Home Coming Service

celebrating the

Fiftieth Anniversary

of the establishment of a
Presbyterian Church in the Glenshaw Valley

Sunday, September 22, 1935

» PROGRAM «

Morning Service, 10:30 o'clock
Rev. Elder D. Crawford, presiding
Rev. Frank J. Bryson, guest speaker
Special Music

Afternoon Service, 3:00 o'clock
I. W. Edgar, presiding
History of the Church and Community and Reminiscing

Evening Service, 8:00 o'clock
Rev. Elder D. Crawford, presiding
Musical Program, under direction H. A. Beiswenger
Rev. W. S. Bingham, guest speaker

General Committee
Rev. Elder D. Crawford   Elton E. Young
Grant Shirk

You and your family are cordially invited
to attend the

DEDICATION SERVICES

of the Renovation recently made in the
Glenshaw Valley Presbyterian Church
including a
New Pipe Organ and Memorial Windows, on
Sunday Morning, January twenty-fifth
at eleven o'clock, and at eight o'clock in the evening.

A Dedicatory Organ Recital

will be given on
Monday Evening, January twenty-sixth
at eight o'clock, by

DR. MARSHALL BIDWELL

Concert Organist and Director of Music
at Carnegie Institute of Pittsburgh.

COMMITTEE

This Glenshaw Christian Education Halloween party took place on October 30, 1917.

In April 1929, the doors of the church were closed and remained closed for two years. A new charter was granted April 15, 1931, under the name Glenshaw Valley Presbyterian Church. This picture shows what the building looked like before remodeling. Notice the gaslights and the railing.

The church was remodeled in 1939. Stained-glass windows were installed, and a new pipe organ was purchased.

Mrs. Bullard is pictured with her class in 1933. From left to right are Elizabeth Engelhardt, Mary Alice Ruchdeschel, Harry Bauer, Doris McKean, Sylvia Ferrari, and Nellie Bright.

This mock wedding took place on June 6, 1933. From left to right are bride Mabel Patz, groom Clara Edgar, Mrs. Schoenman, Mrs. Grubbs, and Alda Ferrari.

Shown here are the attendees of the mock wedding.

Mrs. Shaw and Mrs. Satler are pictured at the church in 1940.

Mrs. Lora Beiswinger, Annie Edgar, Mrs. Hodil, and Mabel O'Hara (from left to right) dressed in old-fashioned clothing for a church benefit in 1940.

This 1940 photograph of Mabel O'Hara was taken at the church benefit.

Edna McMasters, Verna Hunter, and Nancy Young (from left to right) posed for this 1940 photograph at the church benefit.

In this 1940 photograph, pictured on the Shaw front porch are, from left to right: (seated) Dr. Katherine Shaw, Martha Shaw, Mrs. Schoeneman, Marge Hodil, Caroline Shaw Tatom, and Henrietta Schoeneman; (standing) Elizabeth Engelhart and Sara Leight Laubenstein.

In this picture, Elizabeth Engelhardt (left) and Sara Leight Laubenstein (right) are wearing old clothing for a benefit for the Glenshaw Public Library in 1940.

This photograph shows a group of teenagers from the church. From left to right are: Mary Jean Grubbs McMasters, Ruth Ernst, Ruth Bullard, Grace Niggel, Eleanor Carothers Roberts, and Pete McMasters (standing in back).

Pictured here are Grace and Margie Niggel, Sara McMillan, Ann and Edna McMasters, and Margaret Sieg (from left to right).

This is another church event from about 1940.

This photograph of the Ladies Aid Society of Glenshaw Valley Church was taken in the summer of 1946. From left to right are: (seated) Carol Purdy, Nancy Young, Henrietta Schoenemann, unidentified, Jean Hodil, Mary Young, Sarah Louise McMillan, Ann Sieg, Mrs. Ward, Mrs. Elizabeth Engelhardt, and Marjorie Hodil; (standing) Alda Ferrari, Helen McMillan, Mrs. W.B. Gress, unidentified, Mrs. Purdy, Mrs. Eleanor Ernst, Mrs. Feil, Mrs. Annie Satler, unidentified, Mrs. Louise Grant, unidentified, Mrs. Isaac Edgar, Mrs. Kate Seel, Mrs. Helen Hodil, Miss Clara Campbell, Mrs. Ed Seal, unidentified, Mrs. Louis Titzel, Mrs. May Hodil, Mrs. W.L. Shaw, unidentified, and Mrs. Grant Shirk (barely visible on far right).

The women's class of Glenshaw Valley is pictured here. They are, from left to right: Mrs. Stauffer, Mrs. A. Leight, Mrs. Feil, unidentified, Miss Justin, Miss Caton, Mrs. Clendenon, and Miss Davis.

In this photograph of fall cleanup time, *c.* 1929, a kibitzer, John Beiswenger, makes sure that Pete McMasters does a good job.

Sara McMillan (left), Jessie Gerard (right), and Jessie's children are shown as they leave church Bible school on a summer day in 1939.

The actors of the production *'Twas the Night before Christmas* are the subject of this photograph taken in 1942. From left to right are: Pete McMasters, Nancy Young, Carol Purdy, Marjorie Niggel, Virginia Bullard, John Beiswenger, and Jim Sowers.

These people are not digging for gold, but are shoveling out the excess ground. Christian Endeavor members had a ground-breaking ceremony preparatory to concreting the basement floor in 1943. From left to right are: Anne McMasters, Marjorie Niggel, Edna McMasters, and Libs Engelhardt.

Reverend L. Russell Sandy was pastor
of the church from 1939 to 1945.

Wedding bells rang for L. Russell
Sandy and Ruth Hostetter in 1945.

This is the church as it looked in 1943. When the road was paved, the street was raised so that now the porch is even with the road. Earlier pictures show that there were front steps to climb.

Reverend Thomas Cumming (seated) and
Harold Koch (standing) posed for this picture in
1958. They were members of the chorus in a
program for the PTA.

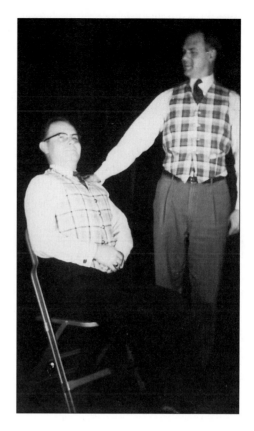

Peg Berneberg (left) and Olive Pearlstein (right)
represented the 1940s in the PTA program held
at the Glenshaw School in 1958.

Bess Clack (left) and Joan Fields (right) dressed in their 1800s outfits for the PTA program.

Marian Pfendler (left) and Joan Fields (right) wore old-fashioned bathing suits when they took part in the program.

Lois Patterson (left) and Vi Rowe (right) dressed in their 1920s outfits.

Here, Olive Pearlstein is pictured in her 1900s dress as she performs in the PTA program.

Lillian Koelsch (left) and Leona Heintz (right) also appeared in the chorus.

Pictured here is the bowling group of the Glenshaw Valley Church in the 1970s. From left to right are: (first row) Pat Engstrom, Lorraine Hieber, Connie Rowe, Gladys Rodenbaugh, Laura Lake, and Bernice Schlarb; (middle row) Ruth Ernst, Vi Rowe, Libs MacDonald, and Shirley Anderson; (back row) Rev. Carl Engstrom, unidentified, Glenn MacDonald, Joe and Anita Beggs, Florence Wagner, Moreland Ernst, George Rodenbaugh, and Jim Guyton.

Three

Industries

This is an 1865 certificate of transfer of Butler Plank Road Stock to Thomas Wilson Shaw.

Shown here is the Beyrleye's ice pond. Henry J. Beyrleye founded the business in 1883 and operated it until his death in 1902. He was assisted by his sons, Henry J. Beyrleye II and Robert J. Beyrleye. The natural ice business continued until 1938.

The horse and wagon carries natural ice from Beyrleye ice pond in this photograph taken in the early twentieth century.

In 1822, Stewart's Lodge was built along the Pittsburgh Butler Turnpike, which is now Mt. Royal Boulevard. The lodge was also known as Pomeroy's Tavern, a stagecoach stop. It was reputed to have been a stop on the Underground Railroad before the demise of slavery. With the passing of the stagecoach era, the acreage was sold to the Armstrong family. They operated it as a successful farm until 1898, when they turned it into Mt. Royal Cemetery. The first burial was in 1904. Stewart's Lodge became the office of the cemetery. On December 6, 1965, fire destroyed the building.

The cemetery built its own stone railroad station on the Pennsylvania and Western railroad in 1902. The station was large enough to contain a chapel, and funeral services could be conducted at the station or at Stewart's Lodge.

This is another view of the cemetery station location, near the railroad, off Butler Plank Road, the site today of the former J & L Warehouse.

This distant view shows the railroad and Butler Plank Road leading to the private station, *c.* 1909. The depot was torn down in 1912.

Shown here is a view of Route 8 from Mt. Royal Cemetery in the 1940s.

This picture is another view of Route 8 from Mt. Royal Cemetery.

This photograph gives a different view of Route 8 from Mt. Royal Cemetery.

This picture was taken looking across Pine Creek and Route 8, toward Glenshaw Glass. The stacks in the background of the photograph are part of a brick-making plant. The picture was taken from the Hunter home.

Mr. Noss and William E. Hunter Sr. had a brick-making plant on Huckleberry Flat (which is now known as Spencer Lane). The Franz brickyard was located south of the present Peoples Gas Company and north of Glenshaw Glass. The plant began operation in 1886. The Wittmer family later operated a yard adjacent to the Gas Company Plant. Its operation was taken over by the Smith brothers from 1901–1910.

In this 1907 photograph, the Glenshaw Glass Company is seen here located on Butler Plank Road (to the right).

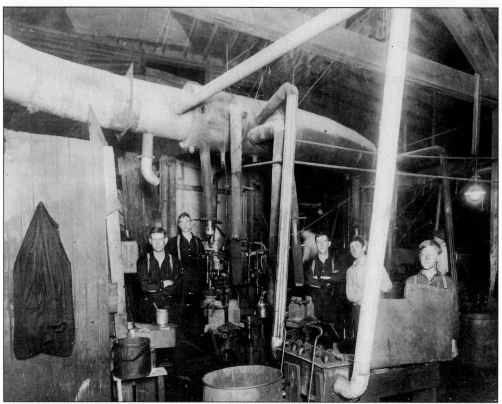

This is a view from inside the Glenshaw Glass plant.

This photograph shows the bottle-making that took place at the Glenshaw Glass plant in the early 1900s.

This is another view of the industries of Glenshaw as they appeared in the early 1900s.

This is Glenshaw Glass as viewed from the hillside above.

This photograph was taken looking up Route 8, where the glass house was later built. Stacks that are seen in the picture are part of the brick plant.

The Ball Chemical Company, owned by Mr. George Ball, was built in 1907 at Wittmer Station, on the property once occupied by the Wittmer Ice Company.

Harry Murray is the second from the left in this view taken from inside the Ball Chemical plant.

Pictured here are employees of Ball Chemical Company. The fourth man from the right is Leroy McElheny, who retired at age 76, after thirty-nine years with the firm.

In 1924, Charlie J. Lang (left) and Nick Turpsic (right) were photographed in Harry Thorn's butcher shop.

Harry Thorn's butcher shop was located on Butler Street, near the May West Bend. Harry Thorn (left) and Charlie Lang (right) are behind the counter.

Harry Thorn and Charlie Lang appear again in this photograph of Thorn's butcher shop.

In this photograph, taken in front of Harry Thorn's butcher shop on Butler Street, Carl Lang is sitting in the back seat.

This was the Thomas Spacing Machine Company, located across Route 8 and north of the Glenshaw Glass Company. The business was established in 1916 and employed one hundred and twenty-five men.

John and Bill Hieber owned Hieber's Garage on Butler Plank Road, near Glenn Avenue. When Route 8 was built, the garage was torn down.

John and Bill Hieber built this garage on Route 8 after their first garage was torn down to make room for the new road. John and his sister, Laura Lake, are standing in the doorway.

The American Natural Gas Company was formed in 1887. In 1925, they disposed of its operating properties to the Columbia Natural Gas Company. This view of the Gas Company includes a partial view of the Cut.

 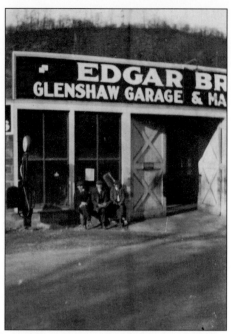

Left: The Elmer J. Nicklas Supply Yard (visible in the background) was established in 1907 by George W. Nicklas, father of the present owner. Pictured across the road, on the grass in the foreground, are Lena Graybrigle Guyton (far right) and son, Jimmy Roy (center), with friends. The post office was built on that site in 1940.
Right: The Edgar Brothers' Garage on Butler Plank Road is shown here. Today, it is the site of Grob's Garage, which is still in operation.

The Ball Chemical Company was built at Wittmer Station, on property once occupied by the Wittmer Ice Company. This fire took place in the 1940s.

Four
Railroad Stations

This is the original Glenshaw Station, built in 1877. It burned down between 1900 and 1905. Seen in the picture are Frank B. McMillan, Isaac Edgar, and Joseph Kay.

This photograph shows the railroad bridge and the original train station.

After the first station burned, this boxcar served as a train station until a new station was built.

This station was built in 1915. When the Busy Beaver Lumber Yard wanted to tear down the station, the Shaler Historical Society started a campaign to move the station to Fall Run Road. In 1976, the station was moved to Fall Run Road, and it was to become a miniature railroad museum, but two months later it burned to the ground.

The Allison Park railroad station is located just north of the Glenshaw Station.

This view of the station shows the four homes on Spencer Lane, as well as the railroad tunnel.

The new B & O station is pictured here. The B & O Railroad abandoned the line in the early 1960s. The Chesapeake & Ohio railroad took over the line, without offering passenger service.

The decorated funeral train of Warren G. Harding, who died August 2, 1923, in San Francisco, was photographed as it passed through Glenshaw on the way to Washington, D.C.

The Glenshaw Station was also decorated for the funeral train of President Harding.

This is a view of the back of the station, which shows the funeral train as it passed by the station and through Glenshaw.

This is a different view of the decorated train station.

The B & O railroad tunnel was photographed while being guarded by soldiers of World War I.

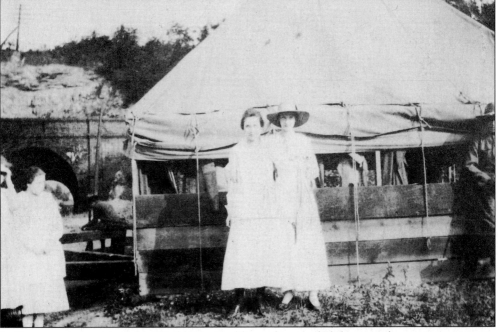

Ladies sometimes visited the World War I soldiers who guarded the tunnel.

Shown here is one of the many train wrecks that took place on the B & O railroad.

This is another view of the train wreck in Glenshaw.

Maryann Beitler, Jean Shearer, and Virginia Miller (from left to right) watch as the train station is getting ready to be moved to Fall Run Road, on March 2, 1976.

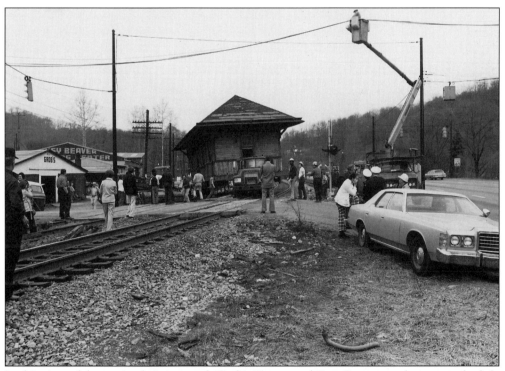

In this view of the station being moved, Grob's Garage and Busy Beaver can be seen to the left. The wires are being lifted so the station can go under them.

The station was moved out to Route 8 for its trip to Fall Run Park. To the right is Nicklas Plumbing Company.

Here, the station is turning off Route 8 to the Fall Run area. This was a major move that took eight hours. The utility companies donated their time.

Going over the bridge in Fall Run was difficult, but the movers made it.

The last B &O passenger train ran in 1950. The line saw no more passenger trains until 1990, when Amtrak started running the Broadway Limited between Chicago, Pittsburgh, and New York City by way of the Glenshaw tracks. Amtrak rerouted the train over different tracks in September 1995. In this photo, the train is passing the actual location where the B & O station stood until 1976. To the left is Fagan's Lumber Yard, formerly Busy Beaver Lumber Yard. Fagan's went out of business about 1995.

Five

Glenshaw School and Library

The Glenshaw Public Library was photographed in 1898 with Ed Crooks Sr. standing at the front door. The library was built as a men's lodge and store. Businessmen in the area bought the building and let the library use the building rent-free. In the 1940s, the library board purchased the building. It is the oldest library east of the Mississippi. Every Friday was library day for the Glenshaw schoolchildren. Each class took turns walking to the library for books.

The Glenshaw School was built in 1889 with four rooms. Four more rooms were added in 1898. In 1900, a two-year high school course was added. To the right is the E.N. Crooks building; the telephone company was located there on the third floor in the 1900s. The building was torn down to make room for a playground for the school. The school is registered with the Pittsburgh History and Landmarks Society.

From left to right are, as listed on the back of the photograph: (front row) Red Bunning, Dudley Campbell, John Titzel, George Edgar, Perry Hunter, and Marvin Phillips; (middle row) Walter Engelhardt, Willard Young, unidentified, Grau Austen, Florence Greenway, Florence McMasters, Florence Phillips, and Howard Auchsenhirt; (back row) Violet Aickson, Rachel Martin, Marg Titzel, Hilda Beiswenger, Hazel Wills, Althea Rector, Elizabeth Shaw, and unidentified.

From left to right are: (front row) Joe Meyers, John Graybrigle, unidentified, Lou Rector, John Titzel, George Edgar, and Perry Hunter; (middle row) Barbara Yost, Mary Kazel Vistein, Laura Hunter, Alda Hunter, Marie Meyers, and unidentified; (back row) Althea Rector, Leila Ochenhirt, Edna Engelhardt, Florence McMasters, Grace Austin, Elizabeth Shaw, Marie Graybrigle, Marg Mau, and unidentified.

Shown here are the Glenshaw School students of 1911–1912. From left to right are: A. Kirk Thompson (teacher); (bottom row) Bill Grob, unidentified, Maurice Meyer, unidentified, Lewis Rector, Clinton Carter, and John Graybrigle; (middle row) Esther Waldschmidt, Lola Smolter, Mae Kletter, Marie Meyer, Edna Engelhardt, Leila Ochenhirt, and Ed Carter; (top row) Mina Smolter, Alda Hunter, Marie Hieber, Elizabeth Mau, and Mabel McKibben.

From left to right are, as listed on the back of the photograph: (front row) Joe Balkey, Charles Balkey, Ray Hunter, Frank Rodenbaugh, Bob Thomas, unidentified, Tom Johnson, Don Craig, and three unidentified; (second row) Francis Phillips, unidentified, Catherine Kletter, Blanch Ebert, Harriet Wylie Thomas, Vera Smolter, Margaret Fay Shaw, Catherine Balkey, ? Kay, five unidentified, Edward Moss, Andrew Engelhardt, ? Engelhardt, Oxenhardt, and Meyer; (third row) five unidentified, ? Wittmer, Louise Seel, and Josephine Wittmer; (fourth row) Miss Sanford; (fifth row) unidentified and Miss Sanders; (sixth row) Mr. Thomson (principal) and Marie Graybrigle; (back row) fourth one in is Pete Kay.

The Glenshaw School students of 1888 are pictured in front of the building at the old Shaw Mill. From left to right are, as listed on the back of the photograph: (front row) Clara Hodil, Sadie Leight, ? Young, John Titzel, unidentified, John McMillan, ? Getting, and Bob McMillan; (second row) Raymond Kelly, unidentified, Jennie Reid, Mabel Harbison, unidentified, unidentified, Alice Harbaugh, Agnes McKibbin, unidentified, Maud Reid, Ellen Harr, Sadie Titzel, and ? Gilmore; (third row) unidentified, Jennie McMillan, Cella Kirk, Annie Marks, unidentified, Annie Kelly, Ida Marks, Bessie Leight, Margaret Harr, ? Gilmore, and Mrs. Young; (fourth row) Bill Reid, Frank Hodil, Albert Kelly, Wade McMillan, Charlie Spencer, ? Young, Bill Harr, and Joe Hodil; (back row) ? Marks, unidentified, Ben Hodil, George White, and Ed Hodil.

This photograph shows recess time at Glenshaw Grade School in the late 1930s. From left to right are: (front row) Mary Young and Edna McMasters; (back row) Jean Hodil, Sarah McMillan, Sam Wiest, Helen Moberg, and Anne McMasters.

This picture was taken on a warm day in the school's side yard. From left to right are: (front row, kneeling) Edna McMasters and Norma Jean Lemay; (middle row, far right) Libs Engelhart standing with Karl Nicklas, who is holding a flag; (back row, second from left) Betty Harr.

Miss Mary Simmons was the librarian of the Glenshaw library from 1913 to 1938. She also sold the first railroad ticket in Glenshaw.

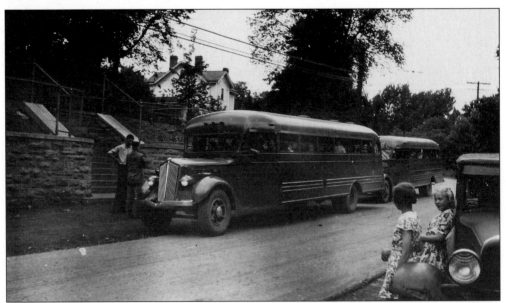

Here, Nellie Bright (left) and Betty Jean Griensen (right) are pictured leaning against a car across the street from Glenshaw School. The stone wall at the school was built by the WPA in the 1930s.

This photograph was taken inside the Glenshaw Public Library. Mrs. M. Mitchell (left) was owner of the doll collection that was on display on April 16, 1946. Mrs. A.W. Ernst (center) was chairman and Catherine Balkey (right) was president of the library board.

Pictured with more dolls on display at the library are, from left to right, Mrs. M. Mitchell (owner of the dolls), Mrs. Ernst (chairman of the of the display), Mrs. Light (librarian), and Catherine Balkey (president of the library board). The library board had purchased the building in 1944.

The library board members are pictured here at an open house on February 6, 1988. After having a new roof installed and the inside of the library painted, the open house was held as a celebration for the new construction. From left to right are: Peg Berneberg (treasurer), three guests, Marie Eichner, Jean Cook, Marsha Sedam Ritter (president), Violet Rowe (librarian), and Olive Pearlstein (secretary).

The new Shaler High School was built on Mt. Royal Boulevard in 1931. In 1951, ground was broken to add on to the old building. The new building was dedicated on February 26, 1953.

This is another view of the high school. An addition was added in 1953. By the 1980s, more space was needed, so a new school was built on Wible Run Road. This building was used as an administration building. The 1996 plans to tear this building down were completed in 1997 for the construction of a new middle school.

This photograph was taken on May Day at Shaler High School in 1941.

Six

Sports

This photograph shows the Glenshaw Marathon that was held in 1909.

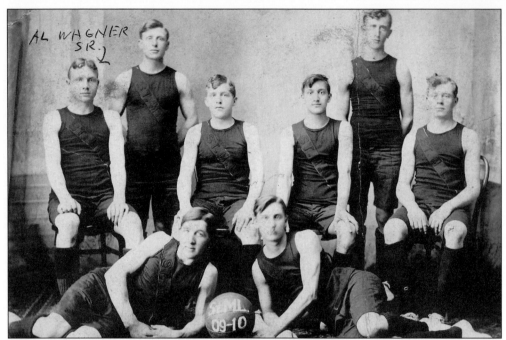

Pictured here is St. Mary's Lyceum basketball team of 1909–1910. Al Wagner Sr. is seated at top left.

This is the Glenshaw basketball team of 1910–1911. From left to right are: (front row) Harvey Leight, Harvey Osborne, and John Mosar; (back row) Arthur Frankenberg, Charles Edgar, Frank Rodenbaugh, and Ernest Kletter.

This is the Glenshaw basketball team of 1911–1912.

The Glenshaw baseball team had their picture taken on May 17, 1921. From left to right are, as listed on the back of the photograph: (front row) Walter Engelhart, Ray Guyton, Jan Ahlbour, Chuck Titzel, Ed Klaus, Carl Marloff, and unidentified; (back row) Bill Graham, Bruce Brozi, and McEllwain.

The All-American team of 1928 is shown here. The man in the middle with the long beard is Dr. Sturgess. He arrived in Glenshaw in 1898. He was an intern at Allegheny General Hospital.

This photograph was taken at the Glenshaw Glass Bowling League picnic in 1933.

"He was definitely out," argued Tas Wagner. Harry "Shade-Tree" Houlihan is the third man from the left. There was "no joy in Mudville" that day, as Glenshaw lost this late 1930s game with Millvale.

Here, "400 O'Hara" swings and misses. Jim often belted the ball up onto the railroad tracks in back of right field. This photograph was taken in the late 1930s.

In 1946, the Glenshaw baseball club showed off their new uniforms, which had been donated by the Syler Manufacturing company. Because Seyler wanted their name prominently displayed on the front of the shirt, there was no room for "Glenshaw."

In the fall of 1946, members of a football team posed for their portrait in front of the Undercliffe Volunteer Fire Company. Shaler Township police officer Rudolph Taylor (far left) was one of the organizers.

Seven
People and Places

Dr. William Sturgess was the first physician
to intern at Allegheny General Hospital,
and he was a family doctor in Glenshaw for
over fifty years. Dr. Sturgess died June 5,
1942, at age 90.

Dr. Katherine Shaw was a physician at Allegheny General Hospital from 1922 to 1938. Dr. Shaw was one of the first female physicians in Allegheny County. She died April 13, 1985, at age 94.

This home on Glenshaw Avenue was built in 1887 and was a twin house to the Satler home next door. Today, it is the home of Sally and John Rowley.

This is John Michael Moran, uncle of Patricia Starr, as he appeared in his World War I uniform.

This photograph of Al Wagner Sr. was taken in 1918, during World War I.

The Shaler branch of the Pittsburgh Chapter of the Red Cross Auxiliary had their picture taken at a parade during World War I.

The Shaler Auxiliary met at the Glenshaw Presbyterian Church during the World War I.

Mrs. A. Happer, the former Hannah Shaw, served in the management department of Cumberland Hospital in Nashville, Tennessee, during the Civil War. After the war, she returned to Glenshaw, where she started the first Sunday school in her brother's home. Later, the Sunday school was moved to the sickle factory. She left Glenshaw in 1870 for Canton, China, where she met and married Dr. Happer and spent the rest of her life in the mission field.

This photograph of the Hunter family was taken in 1916. From left to right are: William E. Hunter, Dale Hunter, William Hunter, Laura Hunter Renick, Perry Hunter, Josephine Hunter, and Alda Hunter Ferrari. Laura Hunter wrote *The History of Glenshaw, 1800–1929*.

The Hunter homestead was located on the hill overlooking the Glenshaw Glass Company.

The Thompson homestead was situated on the hill overlooking Vilsack Road. From left to right are: Elizabeth Thompson, Mildred McElheny Lindner, unidentified, unidentified, and James Thompson.

This group was photographed in front of the haystack on the Thompson homestead. In front of the farmhouse, a natural gas flame burned continuously. Today, a new plan of homes replaced the farm.

Pictured here, from left to right, are: Mr. Showers, Rev. King, Eli McElheny, and William McElheny. McElheny Road is named for the farm that occupied the area.

The Wetzel farmhouse was photographed in 1915. From left to right are, as listed on the back of the photograph: Cara, Marcell, Mr. and Mrs. Wetzel, Kate, George Emig (a hired hand), and Len. Wetzel Road was named for this farm.

Anna Wetzel, George Emig, and Levi Wetzel (from left to right) posed for this portrait on their farm.

Here, the Wetzel family is pictured on their farm. From left to right are: (front row) Al, Mary Lou, and Sylvester Wagner; (back row) Grandma Wetzel and Cecelia and Joe Wagner.

This photograph was taken on the Wetzel farm in 1929. From left to right are: (front row) Sylvester Wagner, Albert Wagner Jr., Leo Goetz, Edward Wetzel Jr., and Ralph Goetz; (middle row) Mary Lou Proft, Clara Wetzel Proft, Anna Nestler Wetzel, Isobel Wetzel, Mary Boucher Wetzel, Marcella Wetzel Goetz, and Alice Goetz; (back row) Albert Wagner Sr., Lois Wagner, Catherine Wetzel Wagner, Sylvester Wetzel, Leonard Wetzel, Anthony Proft, Edward Wetzel Sr., George Emig, George Wetzel, and Helen Wetzel.

In 1932, Cecilia and Joseph Wagner had this photograph taken of themselves.

Mary Ellen Crooks Schrieber posed for this 1935 snapshot.

Here, Clara Hollihan, Mrs. Hack, Emma Crooks, and Mildred Crooks (from left to right) are pictured making apple butter in 1944.

Taking walks on Butler Plank Road was a favorite pastime in the 1930s. Here we see a group of young folks pausing for a rest at the bridge over Pine Creek, near Mr. William's lily pond.

Across the south driveway at Shaler High School, a field was originally located where the Mt. Royal shopping center is now. The field is being plowed by a team of horses in this 1942 photograph.

Mrs. Annie Wallis Satler demonstrated the use of a spinning wheel at a gathering in the summer of 1944.

Elizabeth Birckner (Mrs. William Cook) is pictured here on her one hundredth birthday. She was born November 27, 1868, in Forbach, Lorraine, France. Her great-grandchildren are Willard, Zada Jaspert, Clayton, Marian Repine, and Howard Cook (pictured here from left to right). The Cooks had a son, Henry, who married Marie Meyer, daughter of the late John Jacob Meyer and sister of the president of Glenshaw Glass. The boys were all employed with Glenshaw Glass.

In 1946, Sy and Al Wagner Jr. and George Emig posed for the camera in their uniforms.

A.J. "Pete" McMasters, about the only boy left in town during the war, was an air raid warden. Note the portable siren he is cranking.

This photograph shows people sled riding on Glenshaw Avenue in 1939.

114

Here, John Beiswenger and a group of girls are shown sled riding on Glenshaw Avenue in the late 1930s.

This snow drift, photographed after a winter storm in 1940, had piled up quite high at the Satler front porch.

This view was taken while looking down Glenshaw Avenue on a snowy day.

Elfinwild volunteer firemen posed with their firetruck on the day of the Glenshaw post office dedication in June 1942. The Glenshaw School is visible in the background.

116

When a train whistle blew ten or twenty quick, short blasts, that was the signal that there had been a crossing accident. Such was the case when Chuck Grob's car was struck by the fast mail train that came through Glenshaw in 1939. The wreck was hauled to the side of Grob's Garage for townspeople to view. No one was injured. The car, which had stalled on the tracks, had been borrowed by a man who did odd jobs for the garage. The man ran to the garage to get the tow truck to pull the car off the tracks, but he was too late.

This photograph of a hobo lean-to near Fall Run was taken in 1938.

This aerial view of the valley, taken in 1949, shows the Shaw home (bottom right), another Shaw house (middle), and the Schrieber home (upper left).

George V. Beitler, in the middle of the photograph, was appointed postmaster of the Glenshaw post office in May 1949. At his left is Arthur Bloomer of the Allison Park post office, and to his right is Leslie Carlisle of the Verona post office.

The Glenshaw Story was presented at Scott Junior High School in July 1976. From left to right, the chorus members were, as listed on the back of the photograph: (front row) Jan Kumpfmiller, Vickie Lynch, unidentified, Debbie Ruby, Julie Zsoldas, unidentified, and Jean Jack; (back row) Carol Brinjak, unidentified, Jennie Rupert, Virginia Miller, unidentified, Erma Kearney, unidentified, Charlie Gray, Fred Gray, Ralph George, Don Gradkowski, and David Beall.

Here, Sylvia Moran is modeling a dress of the 1950s for *The Glenshaw Story*.

In this photograph, Sandy Anderson is modeling her Civil War dress. The narrator, Violet Rowe, is visible to the right.

These models are portraying the three Glenshaw telephone operators, Dolly Wright, Fern Harm, and Della Shorthill, in this segment of *The Glenshaw Story*.

121

Here, Pam (left) and Virinia (right) Moran are shown playing basketball in the 1920s.

This photograph shows Pam Moran wearing a gown of the 1800s.

For this photograph, Maryann Beitler wore one of the outfits from the Shaw collection, a purple wool skating outfit from the 1900s.

This photograph shows another train wreck that took place at the Glenshaw crossing.

The Allegheny County commissioners, Bob Forester (far left), Leonard C. Staisey (center, holding a drawing of the train station), and William R. Hunt (far right), commended the committee of the Historical Society for their effort to move the station. Pictured are, from left to right, La Rue B. Dorrell, Mary Ann Beitler, Virginia Miller, and Jean Shearer.

This eleven-room house on Mt. Royal Boulevard was built about 1830 by Captain James Shaw, a ferryboat captain. The house also served as a roadhouse, and guests stayed on the third floor. It was partially destroyed by fire and rebuilt in 1868. It is also registered with the Pittsburgh History and Landmarks Foundation.

This photograph of the Edward Crooks property, located between 1600 and 1544 Butler Plank Road, was taken prior to 1937.

This is another view, almost at the same angle, looking at Edward Crooks's property; however, the top soil has been removed.

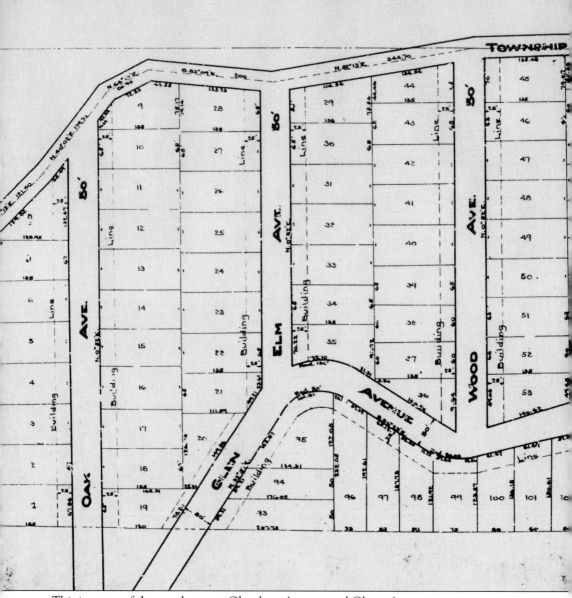

This is a map of the area between Glenshaw Avenue and Glenn Avenue.

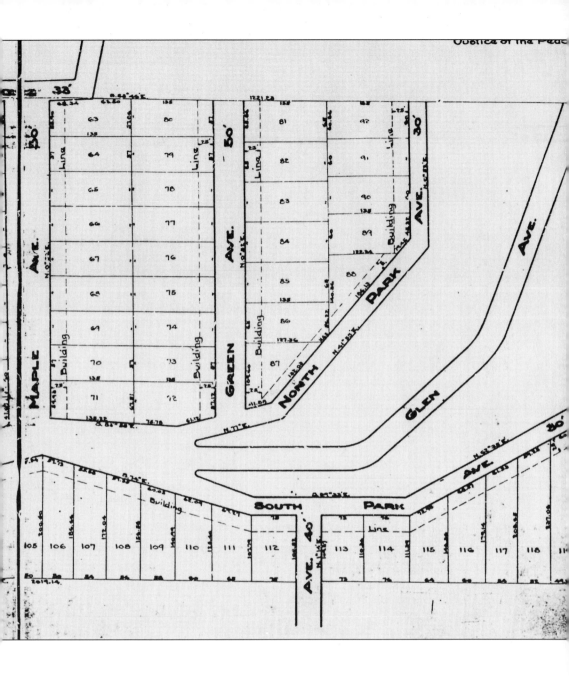

Shown here is the Historic Landmark plaque on the Glenshaw Valley Presbyterian Church. The plaque was stolen from the church in 1976.

This photograph shows the Hunter's home on Route 8. The bridge at left crosses Pine Creek. The area behind the house is bare of trees as a result of logging.